Writing Skills & Grammar

Written by Dona Herweck Rice

Teacher Created Materials, Inc.
P.O. Box 1040
Huntington Beach, CA 92647
©1997 Teacher Created Materials, Inc.
Made in U.S.A.

ISBN 1-57690-247-1

Illustrator:
Sue Fullam
Myron Grossman

Cover Artist:
Chris Macabitas

Editor:
Karen Goldfluss, M.S. Ed.

Imaging:
Ralph Olmedo, Jr.
James Edward Grace

Note to Parents and Teachers:

The books in this series were designed to help parents and teachers reinforce basic skills for their children and students. *Writing Skills & Grammar* reviews basic writing and grammar skills for the third grade level. The exercises in this book can be done sequentially or can be taken out of order, as needed. In order to complete all exercises, children will need a pencil and crayons.

Here are some useful ideas for making the most of the books in this series.

- Remove the answer key and keep it for your own use.

- Help beginning readers with the instructions.

- Review the work the child has done. Whenever possible, work with the child.

- Allow the child to use whatever writing instruments he or she prefers. For example, colored pencils can add variety and pleasure to drill work.

- Pay attention to the areas in which the child has the most difficulty. Provide extra guidance and exercises in those areas.

Name _____

Read each sentence. Write the word from the word box that means **the same thing as** the underlined word.

Let's **gather** some leaves for our art project.

Let's **collect** some leaves for our art project.

asked	bucket	eat	shore	small
big	decorate	quiet	slept	watched

_____ 1. The Martians <u>observed</u> the people of Earth.

_____ 2. The waves roll upon the <u>beach.</u>

_____ 3. We will <u>dine</u> at a nearby restaurant.

_____ 4. The children filled the <u>pail</u> with sand.

_____ 5. After playing, we all <u>napped</u> for awhile.

_____ 6. The teacher <u>questioned</u> the students about their homework.

_____ 7. In December, some people <u>trim</u> a tree.

_____ 8. The insects were <u>tiny.</u>

_____ 9. A <u>large</u> storm is coming our way.

_____ 10. Everyone was <u>silent.</u>

Name _____

Read each sentence. Write the word from the word box that means the **opposite** of the underlined word.

The lady **laughed** as she watched the movie.

The lady **cried** as she watched the movie.

bad	difficult	empty	few	no one
calm	down	everybody	low	white

_____ 1. The leaf was too <u>high</u> to reach.

_____ 2. The bag was <u>full.</u>

_____ 3. The sun was <u>up</u> when we left.

_____ 4. <u>Many</u> people listen to the radio.

_____ 5. The drill team was dressed all in <u>black.</u>

_____ 6. The students thought the test was <u>easy.</u>

_____ 7. <u>Nobody</u> came to the play.

_____ 8. <u>Someone</u> is coming to party.

_____ 9. The sea was <u>wild.</u>

_____ 10. Everyone had a <u>good</u> time at the show.

Name _____

A noun names

a person,   place,   or thing.

Underline each noun.

1. The dancer jumped in the air.

2. The boy watched television.

3. Mr. Smith teaches our class.

4. The baby cried for its mother.

5. The sisters walked to the store.

6. My school has two stories.

7. The teenagers rode their skateboards through the park.

8. The dentist treated a new patient.

9. A little dog picked a fight with a big cat.

10. There were presents, cake, and candles at my birthday party.

Name _____

8

Jim **ate eight**
slices of
pizza today!

Choose the correct word to use in each sentence.

pail   pale   1. They collected sea shells in the_____.

Two   To   2. _____friends went to the concert.

here   hear   3. Do you_____that noise?

wear   where   4. I am going to_____my new sweater.

so   sew   5. He will have to_____his button onto his
shirt.

hi   high   6. The snow fell_____in the mountains.

wood   would   7. Collect some_____for the fire.

be   bee   8. A honey_____flew to the hive.

blew   blue   9. The wind_____across the water.

knew   new   10. I_____you would come!

Name _____

Some of the words below are spelled correctly and some are not.
Correct the misspelled words.

1. cloo _____   11. fich _____

2. shake _____   12. cookey _____

3. row _____   13. monkie _____

4. lin _____   14. donkey _____

5. freze _____   15. name _____

6. bote _____   16. eech _____

7. sayl _____   17. lowd _____

8. march _____   18. gurl _____

9. tea _____   19. boy _____

10. womin _____   20. loe _____

Name _____

Match each noun to a verb.

dog	twinkles
bird	meows
cat	gallops
horse	learn
star	play
sun	sings
students	barks
children	shines

ring sparkles

(noun   (verb)

The ruby ring sparkles in the sunlight.

Write a sentence for each noun/verb pair above.

1. _____

2. _____

3. _____

4. _____

5. _____

6. _____

7. _____

8. _____

Name _____

A verb shows action.

The car **struggled** up the hill.

The car **sped** down the hill.

Write the verbs on the lines.

1. Barbara plays basketball well. _____

2. The bird flies over my head. _____

3. The bicycle makes Frank happy. _____

4. The children ran to the playground. _____

5. The balloon popped in front of me. _____

6. The pen ran out of ink. _____

7. I fell on the sidewalk. _____

8. I eat a piece of fruit each day. _____

9. The old horse stood quietly in the field. _____

10. Our teacher reads a story to us each day. _____

Name _____

The subject of a sentence is **who** or **what** the sentence is about.

The predicate is what the subject **does, has,** or **is.**

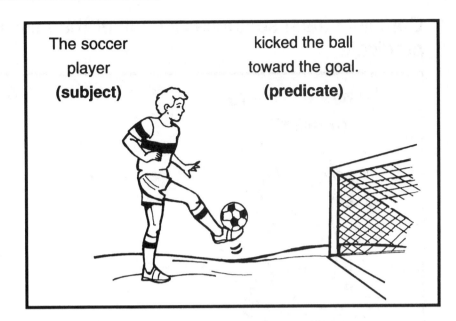

The soccer player
(subject)

kicked the ball toward the goal.
(predicate)

Fill in a subject for each sentence below.

1. _____exploded.

2. _____is beautiful.

3. _____tripped over my foot.

4. _____laughed loudly.

5. _____should have gone to class.

Fill in a predicate for each sentence below.

1. Our teacher_____.

2. This movie_____.

3. The gray cat _____.

4. My grandmother _____.

5. The table _____.

Name _____

Complete each sentence with either the missing subject or the missing predicate.

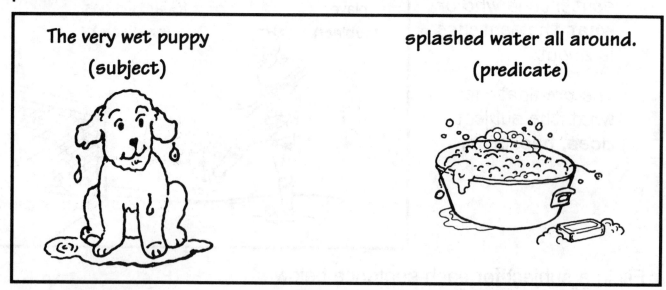

The very wet puppy
(subject)

splashed water all around.
(predicate)

1. The rabbit _____.

2. _____ wore an old shoe.

3. A friendly mouse _____.

4. _____ caught fire.

5. _____ played by the river.

6. My best friend _____.

7. _____ sang a song.

8. _____ climbed over the fence.

9. The girl across the street _____.

10. _____ ate the box of cereal.

Name _____

When subjects and verbs are together in a sentence, they must agree in number.

The sandal (fit, (fits)) well.

A **singular subject** (only one) takes a singular verb.

A **plural subject** (more than one) takes a plural verb.

Circle the correct singular or plural verb. Write the word **singular or plural** after each sentence.

1. The rabbit (hops, hop). _____

2. The sun (shines, shine). _____

3. The cakes (was, were) delicious. _____

4. Angry tigers (roars, roar) loudly. _____

5. The man (rides, ride) his bike to work. _____

6. Winter vacation (is, are) coming soon. _____

7. The boys (has, have) red shirts. _____

8. The flowers (is, are) blooming. _____

9. Karen (dances, dance) very well. _____

10. The tomatoes (is, are) ripe. _____

Name _____

The sentences below are complete because they each have a subject and a predicate. However, they are the simplest sentences possible. Add words to each sentence to make it more interesting. An example has been done for you.

Boy walks.

The small, tired boy walks slowly to his bed and climbs inside the covers.

---

1. Girl disappeared.

_____

_____

2. Horses galloped.

_____

_____

3. Dishes broke.

_____

_____

4. Radio plays.

_____

_____

5. Motorcycle roared.

_____

_____

6. Artist paints.

_____

_____

Name _____

Unscramble these words to make a sentence.

1. bananas eat gorillas ripe

   _____

2. the door opened magician secret the

   _____

3. sense this makes sentence

   _____

4. broke the on egg my head

   _____

5. the nap a took dog tired

   _____

6. zookeeper bit the snake the

   _____

7. his pencil sharpened the boy

   _____

8. for computer the girl a her program made

   _____

9. mother called I phone my the on

   _____

10. the television watched Susie

    _____

Name _____

Every predicate must contain a verb. Usually the predicate contains more than a verb. These extra words are called a **complement**. A complement is a word or group of words that complete the sense of the predicate.

> **The rabbit blinked.**
> **The rabbit blinked at me through the bushes.**

Add a complement to the sentence parts below. An example has been done for you.

1. The crowd screamed

_____

_____

2. Joe enjoys

_____

_____

3. My brother borrowed

_____

_____

4. Terry ate

_____

_____

5. A winter morning is

_____

_____

6. The pilot flew

_____

_____

Name _____

An adjective
describes people,
places, and things.

a
diamond
ring

many   **loose**   **funny**   **large**   **striped**

Use the words in boldface to add an adjective to each sentence.

1. The _____ zebra is a beautiful animal.

2. My clothes are baggy and _____.

3. _____ people watch television each day.

4. We laughed at the _____ movie.

5. The giant was so _____ he blocked the sun
   when he stood.

Add an adjective to each sentence below.

6. The monkeys swing from the trees.

   _____

7. The owl hooted in the night.

   _____

8. The farmer plants his crops.

   _____

9. Have you seen my shoes?

   _____

10. A hummingbird flew past the window.

   _____

Name _____

A sentence fragment is an incomplete sentence. It is missing either the subject or the predicate, and it does not make sense by itself.

The tired horse **(fragment)**

The tired horse moved slowly across the meadow. **(sentence)**

Make the fragments below into complete sentences.

1. the hungry bear

_____

_____

2. chews gum loudly

_____

_____

3. the mountains

_____

_____

4. my first birthday party

_____

_____

5. danced all night

_____

_____

6. the gigantic elephant

_____

_____

7. is my favorite present

_____

_____

Name _____

In the box there are four complete sentences and three fragments.
Rewrite the sentences adding capitals and ending punctuation.
Rewrite the fragments adding either subjects or predicates.

1. i have many things in my room
2. there is a box of clothes under the bed
3. a rug is in front of the closet
4. two stuffed rabbits
5. i can see trees from my window
6. the bedspread and curtains
7. a large poster of

1. _____

_____

2. _____

_____

3. _____

_____

4. _____

_____

5. _____

_____

6. _____

_____

7. _____

_____

Name _____

Read the story below. Add the missing punctuation.

Have you ever been on a farm

Mrs Young took her third grade class to Mr Frank s

farm on Tuesday, February third, in the morning

They saw cows chickens and horses Mr Frank

wanted to know if any students would like to ride a

horse Leslie screamed I do Also John and Carl

wanted to ride Mrs Young s class will never forget

the special day on the farm

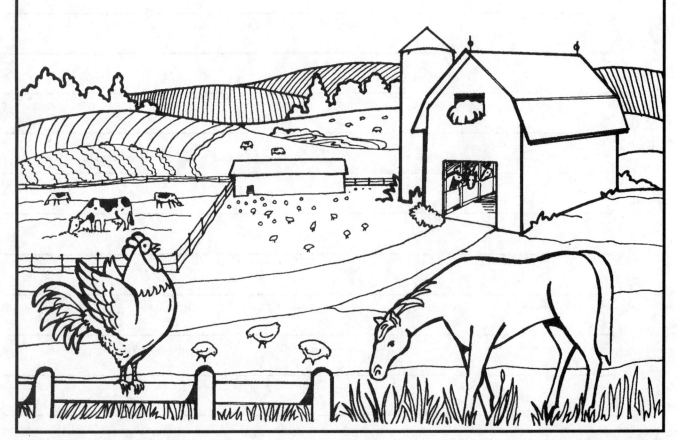

Name _____

Write a contraction for each set of words.

1. can not _____

2. he is _____

3. will not _____

4. does not _____

5. they are _____

6. we are _____

7. should not _____

8. it will _____

would not= wouldn't

Write the words that make the contraction.

9. she'll _____

10. it's _____

11. mustn't _____

12. you're _____

13. they'll _____

14. haven't _____

15. I'll _____

16. I'm _____

we'll= we will

Write two sentences. Use at least one contraction in each.

_____

_____

_____

_____

Name _____

Write a sentence for each word. Be sure to capitalize the beginning and to add punctuation to the end.

laugh   1. _____

_____

wonder   2. _____

_____

man   3. _____

_____

leaf   4. _____

_____

bun   5. _____

_____

color   6. _____

_____

mop   7. _____

_____

dream   8. _____

_____

tiny   9. _____

_____

is   10. _____

_____

Name _____

was? were? does? do?

He **was** playing.

They **were** playing.

She **does** her chores.

They **do** their chores.

Write **was** or **were** in each sentence.

1. Where_____we supposed to meet?

2. Who_____with you?

3. I_____at school when the siren sounded.

4. We_____watching a play.

5. She_____confused about the homework.

6. They_____wondering where to go.

Write **do** or **does** in each sentence.

7. Where_____you keep the sugar?

8. I will_____the dishes.

9. They will_____the laundry after we leave.

10. She_____her best on all her work.

11. Kevin_____a good job when he hoes the garden.

12. Who_____the paperwork in the office?

Name _____

The words below are written in the present tense (today). On the blank after each word, write its form in the past tense (before today). The first one has been done for you.

(present)

paint

(past)

painted

1. paint ___painted___

2. climb _____

3. play _____

4. laugh _____

5. shout _____

6. jump _____

7. run _____

8. see _____

9. eat _____

10. come _____

11. make _____

12. build _____

13. sleep _____

14. give _____

15. take _____

16. bring _____

17. sing _____

18. hold _____

19. go _____

20. write _____

Name _____

The monkey chatters **noisily.**
(How)

Adverbs are describing words that tell when (a time), where (a place), or how (how something is done).

Underline the adverbs. On the lines, write **how, where,** or **when** to show the way in which the adverb is used.

_____ 1. I walked quietly.

_____ 2. We will go tomorrow.

_____ 3. We can play later.

_____ 4. My cousins will come here.

_____ 5. The cheetah growled fiercely.

_____ 6. The mother sang softly.

_____ 7. The ballerina dances gracefully.

_____ 8. Yesterday I played baseball.

_____ 9. The orchestra played well.

_____10. He completed his homework quickly.

Name _____

Read the words that are being compared. Fill in each blank with the
best word from the word box.

Cat is to **pet**   as   **Car** is to **vehicle**

bird	goal	night	skin	winter
draw	head	quack	swim	year

1. Chicken is to cluck as duck is to_____.

2. Banana is to peel as apple is to _____.

3. Football is to touchdown as hockey is to _____.

4. Bird is to fly as fish is to _____.

5. Leaf is to tree as feather is to_____.

6. Pencil is to write as crayon is to _____.

7. Light is to day as dark is to_____.

8. Day is to week as month is to_____.

9. Hot is to summer as cold is to _____.

10. Roof is to house as hat is to_____.

Name _____

A **cause** is the reason why something happens. The **effect** is what happens.

Read each cause. Write an effect.

1. The class had perfect attendance. _____
_____

2. The monkey ate all the bananas. _____
_____

3. The girl forgot her homework. _____
_____

4. The clock stopped ticking. _____
_____

Read each effect. Write a cause.

5. There was a traffic jam on the highway. _____
_____

6. Ice cream spilled on the floor. _____
_____

7. The baby started to cry. _____
_____

8. Everyone shouted, "Hooray!"_____
_____

Name _____

An apostrophe is used to show ownership (possession) in writing. For example, to write **toy belonging to baby,** one can write **baby's toy.**

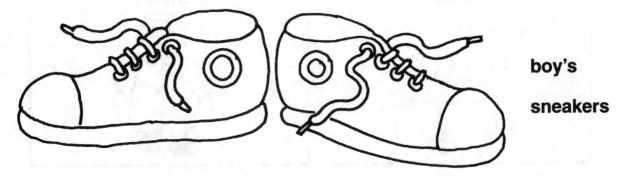

boy's

sneakers

Rewrite the phrases below using an **'s.** (Note: If the word ends in **s,** only add an apostrophe.)

1. food belonging to a cat _____

2. nest belonging to a bird_____

3. bike belonging to Kenny _____

4. store belonging to Mr. Stout _____

5. radio belonging to Janie _____

6. book belonging to Don _____

7. baseball belonging to the coach _____

8. desk belonging to the teacher_____

9. closet belonging to the class _____

10. pencil belonging to Mrs. Davis _____

Name _____

Rewrite these dates and addresses using a comma correctly.

1. April 15 1972 _____

2. July 27 1640 _____

3. September 13 1910 _____

4. Monday January 31 _____

5. Sunday November 16 _____

6. Anaheim California _____

7. Albuquerque New Mexico _____

8. Quebec Canada _____

9. Bangor Maine _____

10. Little Rock Arkansas _____

Use a comma correctly in these letter parts.

11. Dear Joe _____

12. Your friend _____

13. Sincerely yours _____

14. Love _____

15. Yours truly _____

Add commas where they are needed in these sentences.

16. All birds have feathers wings and beaks.

17. The Shetland pony is small friendly and gentle.

18. A friendly playful dog makes a good pet.

19. I have three cats named Boots Muffin and Tiger.

20. I like to color with pencils markers and crayons.

Name _____

Write an invitation to a party you would like to have. Color and
decorate the invitation as well.

Name _____

Write a thank you letter to someone for something you have received.
Color and decorate the letter as well.

_____ (top right)

_____ (date/greeting line)

_____

_____

_____

_____

_____

_____

_____

_____

_____ (closing)

_____ (signature)

Name _____

A **paragraph** is a group of sentences that tells about one topic. The
sentences in a paragraph should be written in order.

On the lines below, write a paragraph, using the words provided for
the first word in each sentence.

Imagine that you are the teacher for a day. What will you do in
your classroom?

If I was teacher for a day, first _____

_____

_____

Next, _____

_____

_____

Then, _____

_____

_____

Finally, _____

_____

_____

_____

_____

Answer Key

Page 2
1. watched
2. shore
3. eat
4. bucket
5. slept
6. asked
7. decorate
8. small
9. big
10. quiet

Page 3
1. low
2. empty
3. down
4. few
5. white
6. difficult
7. everybody
8. no one
9. calm
10. bad

Page 4
1. dancer; air
2. boy; television
3. Mr. Smith; class
4. baby; mother
5. sisters; store
6. school; stories
7. teenagers; skateboards; park
8. dentist; patient
9. dog; fight; cat
10. presents; cake; candles; party

Page 5
1. pail
2. Two
3. hear
4. wear
5. sew
6. high
7. wood
8. bee
9. blew

10. knew

Page 6
1. clue
2. correct
3. correct
4. line
5. freeze
6. boat
7. sail
8. correct
9. correct
10. woman
11. fish
12. cookie
13. monkey
14. correct
15. correct
16. each
17. loud
18. girl
19. correct
20. low

Page 7
dog - barks
bird - sings
cat - meows
horse - gallops
star - twinkles
sun - shines
students - learn
children - play
Sentences will vary.

Page 8
1. plays
2. flies
3. makes
4. ran
5. popped
6. ran
7. fell
8. eat
9. stood
10. reads

Page 9
Sentences will vary.

Page 10
Sentences will vary.

Page 11
1. hops; singular
2. shines; singular
3. were; plural
4. roar; plural
5. rides; singular
6. is; singular
7. have; plural
8. are; plural
9. dances; singular
10. are; plural

Page 12
Sentences will vary.

Page 13
1. Gorillas eat ripe bananas.
2. The magician opened the secret door.
3. This sentence makes sense.
4. The egg broke on my head.
5. The tired dog took a nap.
6. The snake bit the zookeeper.
7. The boy sharpened his pencil.
8. The girl made a program for her computer.
9. I called my mother on the phone.
10. Susie watched the television.

Page 14
Sentences will vary.

Page 15
1. striped
2. loose
3. Many

4. funny
5. large
Sentences 6-10 will vary.

Page 16
Sentences will vary.

Page 17
1. I have many things in my room.
2. There is a box of clothes under the bed.
3. A rug is in front of the closet.
4. Fragment; sentences will vary.
5. I can see trees from my window.
6. Fragment; sentences will vary.
7. Fragment; sentences will vary.
8. Fragment; sentences will vary.
9. I keep my room neat and clean.
10. Fragment; sentences will vary.

Page 18
Have you ever been on a farm?
Mrs. Young took her third grade class to Mr. Frank's farm on Tuesday, February third, in the morning. They saw cows, chickens, and horses. Mr. Frank wanted to

Answer Key *(cont.)*

know if any students would like to ride a horse. Leslie screamed, "I do!" Also, John and Carl wanted to ride. Mrs. Young's class will never forget the special day on the farm.

Page 19
1. can't
2. he's
3. won't
4. doesn't
5. they're
6. we're
7. shouldn't
8. it'll
9. she will
10. it is
11. must not
12. you are
13. they will
14. have not
15. I will
16. I am

Page 20
Sentences will vary.

Page 21
1. were
2. wasp
3. was
4. were
5. was
6. were
7. do
8. do
9. do
10. does
11. does
12. does

Page 22
1. painted
2. climbed
3. played
4. laughed
5. shouted
6. jumped
7. ran

8. saw
9. ate
10. came
11. made
12. built
13. slept
14. gave
15. took
16. brought
17. sang
18. held
19. went
20. wrote

Page 23
1. quietly–how
2. tomorrow–when
3. later–when
4. here–where
5. fiercely–how
6. softly–how
7. gracefully–how
8. Yesterday–when
9. well–how
10. quickly–how

Page 24
1. quack
2. skin
3. goal
4. swim
5. bird
6. color
7. night
8. year
9. winter
10. head

Page 25
Causes and effects will vary.

Page 26
1. cat's food
2. bird's nest
3. Kenny's bike
4. Mr. Stout's store
5. Janie's radio
6. Don's book
7. coach's baseball
8. teacher's desk

9. class' closet
10. Mrs. Davis' pencil

Page 27
1. April 15, 1972
2. July 27, 1640
3. September 13, 1910
4. Monday, January 31
5. Sunday, November 16
6. Anaheim, California
7. Albuquerque, New Mexico
8. Quebec, Canada
9. Bangor, Maine
10. Little Rock, Arkansas
11. Dear Joe,
12. Your friend,
13. Sincerely yours,
14. Love,
15. Yours truly,
16. All birds have feathers, wings, and beaks.
17. The Shetland pony is small, friendly, and gentle.
18. A friendly, playful dog makes a good pet.
19. I have three cats named Boots, Muffin, and Tiger.
20. I like to color with pencils, markers, and crayons.

Page 28
Invitations will vary.

Page 29
Letters will vary.

Page 30
Paragraphs will vary.